RITER: **MARK MILLAR**

RTIST: **STEVE McNIVEN**

KS: **DEXTER VINES**

ITH **MARK MORALES, STEVE McNIVEN,
JHN DELL & TIM TOWNSEND**

LOUR: **MORRY HOLLOWELL**

TTERS: **CHRIS ELIOPOULOS**

VER ART: **STEVE MCNIVEN**

RIANT COVERS: **MICHAEL TURNER & ASPEN**

RODUCTION: **KATE LEVIN & RICH GINTER**

SISTANT EDITORS: **MOLLY LAZER &
JBREY SITTERSON**

SOCIATE EDITOR: **ANDY SCHMIDT**

ITOR: **TOM BREVOORT**

ITOR IN CHIEF: **JOE QUESADA**

BLISHER: **DAN BUCKLEY**

ECIAL THANKS TO **LAURA MARTIN, DAVE McCAIG,
AUL MOUNTS, WIL QUINTANA & ANDREW CROSSLEY**

CIVIL WAR

you have any comments or queries about this graphic novel? Email us at graphicnovels@panini.co.uk. Find us on Facebook @Panini/Marvel Graphic Novels.

TM & © 2006, 2007 and 2015 Marvel & Subs. Licensed by Marvel Characters B.V. through Panini S.p.A, Italy. All Rights Reserved. First
printing 2007. 26th impression 2015. Published by Panini Publishing, a division of Panini UK Limited. Mike Riddell, Managing Director.
Alan O'Keefe, Managing Editor. Mark Irvine, Production Manager. Marco M. Lupoi, Publishing Director Europe. Brady Webb, Reprint
Editor. Angela Gray, Designer. Office of publication: Brockbourne House, 77 Mount Ephraim, Tunbridge Wells, Kent TN4 8BS. This
publication may not be sold, except by authorised dealers, and is sold subject to the condition that it shall not be sold or distributed
with any part of its cover or markings removed, nor in a mutilated condition. Printed in Italy by Terrazzi. ISBN: 978-1-905239-60-3

CIVIL

WAR

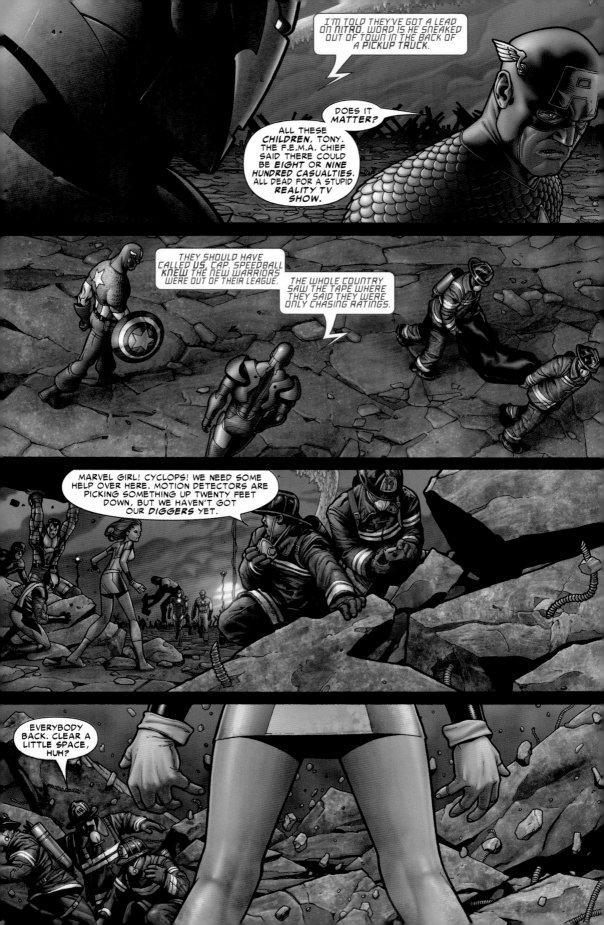

A BAN ON SUPER HEROES? WELL, IN A WORLD WITH THOUSANDS OF SUPER-VILLAINS THAT'S OBVIOUSLY IMPOSSIBLE, LARRY.

BUT TRAINING THEM UP AND MAKING THEM CARRY BADGES? YES, I'D SAY THAT SOUNDS LIKE A REASONABLE RESPONSE.

...AND SO WE ASK YOU, LORD, FOR YOUR MERCY. NOT ONLY FOR THE SOULS OF THE CHILDREN WHO PERISHED, BUT FOR THE SUPER-PEOPLE WHOSE CARELESSNESS *CAUSED* THIS TRAGEDY.

TONY STARK?

WHAT?

MAN, YOU GOT A *NERVE* SWAGGERING AROUND TOWN AFTER *THAT*. I WAS YOU, I'D BE ASHAMED TO *GO OUTSIDE*.

HELL ARE YOU *SHRIEKING* ABOUT, TUBBY? I GOT NOTHING TO DO WITH SPEEDBALL OR THE NEW WARRIORS. THOSE GUYS WERE C-LIST, TOPS.

BABY-KILLER!

JOHNNY, I DON'T *LIKE* THIS. I WANT TO GO HOME.

KLEEESH!

HNNY!

HOLD HIM DOWN! HOLD HIM DOWN!

--HUMAN TORCH, THE LATEST IN A SERIES OF ATTACKS ON NEW YORK'S SUPER-COMMUNITY. MORE AT ELEVEN, PLUS THE GROWING PRESSURE ON THE PRESIDENT--

--THE PEOPLE OF STAMFORD ASK: WHAT ARE HIS PROPOSALS FOR SUPER HERO REFORM?

BRYAN DEEMER

THE BAXTER BUILDING:

SO WHAT ARE THEY SAYING, DOCTOR RICHARDS?

THAT I'LL BE FORCED TO BECOME A *FEDERAL EMPLOYEE* OR FACE A WARRANT FOR MY *ARREST*?

ACTUALLY, YOU WERE ONE OF THE FEW *POST-HUMANS* THEY'RE HOPING TO SEEK A *COMPROMISE* WITH, STEPHEN.

PENSION PLANS AND *ANNUAL VACATION TIME*? IT'S *RIDICULOUS*. WHAT ARE THEY TRYING TO DO? TURN US INTO *CIVIL SERVANTS*?

LOOKS TO ME LIKE THEY'RE *CLOSING US DOWN*, WASP.

CAPTAIN.

COMMANDER HILL.

I'M TOLD THAT TWENTY-THREE OF YOUR FRIENDS ARE MEETING IN THE BAXTER BUILDING RIGHT NOW TO DISCUSS HOW THE SUPER-PEOPLE SHOULD RESPOND TO THE PRESIDENT'S BIG SOLUTION.

YOU THINK THEY'RE GOING TO GO FOR IT?

I DON'T THINK THAT'S FOR ME TO JUDGE.

C'MON, ROGERS. CUT THE CRAP. WE'RE NEVER GOING TO BE TIGHT LIKE YOU AND NICK FURY, BUT I'M STILL THE ACTING HEAD OF S.H.I.E.L.D.

RESPECT THE BADGE IF NOTHING ELSE.

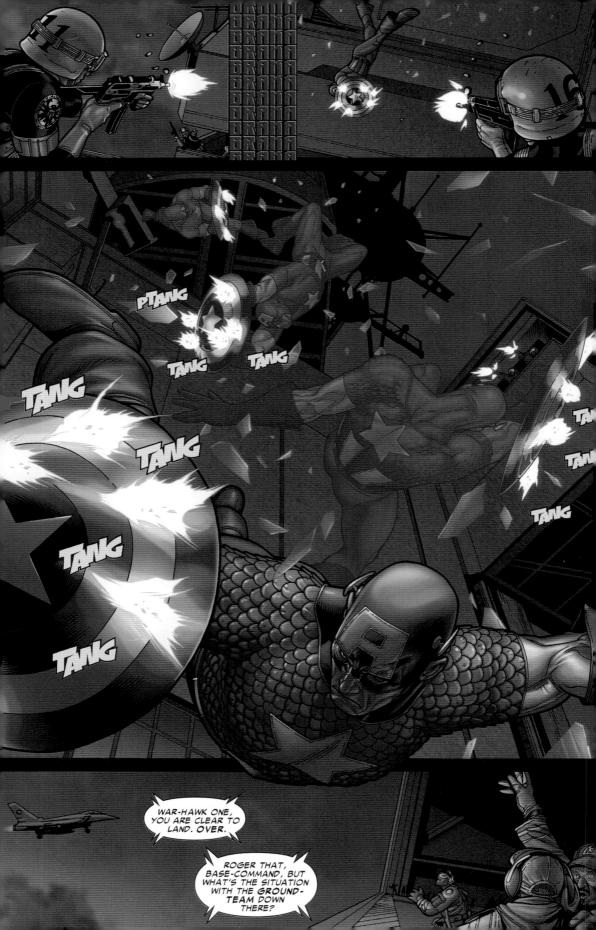

NO, THE FACT THAT CONGRESS HAS RESPONDED SO SWIFTLY JUST PROVES WHAT AN EFFECTIVE POLITICAL OPERATOR MIRIAM SHARPE HAS BECOME.

SHE AND THE OTHER STAMFORD REFORMISTS HAVE REALLY TAPPED INTO AMERICA'S QUIET DISCOMFORT WITH SUPERHUMAN MISBEHAVIOR HERE...

...AND THEN HE LANDED THE JET IN A FOOTBALL FIELD BEFORE TAKING THE PILOT FOR A HAMBURGER AND FRIES.

AIN'T THAT JUST LIKE CAPTAIN AMERICA? MAKING SURE A TWO-BILLION-DOLLAR WARPLANE DON'T GET DAMAGED NO MATTER HOW MUCH TROUBLE HE'S IN?

I'M GLAD YOU THINK THIS IS FUNNY, MISTER SECRETARY, BECAUSE I WAS UNDER THE IMPRESSION THAT OUR REGISTRATION PLAN WAS CONTROVERSIAL ENOUGH.

THE BAXTER BUILDING, HOME OF THE FANTASTIC FOUR:

HOW'S *THE PROJECT* COMING ALONG, REED?

LIKE A DREAM. TONY'S BIG PLAN FOR THE SUPERHUMAN COMMUNITY IS THE MOST EXCITING THING WE'VE EVER WORKED ON, SUE.

HE WASN'T KIDDING WHEN HE SAID HE'D REVOLUTIONIZE EVERY META-HUMAN IN AMERICA. I HAVEN'T BEEN THIS *EXCITED* SINCE I SAW MY FIRST BLACK HOLE.

YEAH, WELL. MAYBE I'D BE EXCITED *TOO* IF HIS GENIUS PLAN DIDN'T MEAN JAIL FOR HALF OUR *CHRISTMAS CARD LIST.*

AGREED. BUT THEY DON'T LEAVE US ANY CHOICE IF THEY REFUSE TO *REGISTER*, HONEY. JUST TAKE A LOOK AT MY PROJECTIONS IF YOU NEED TO SEE THE *SOCIAL DANGERS* THEY'RE CREATING.

WHY DO WE NEED NEW SECRET IDENTITIES?

YOUR OLD ONES ARE PROBABLY COMPROMISED, PATRIOT, AND YOU'RE GOING TO NEED *SOMEWHERE* TO HIDE WHEN WE AREN'T OUT THERE KICKING ASS AND TAKING NAMES.

THIS IS WHERE WE LIVE FOR THE *DURATION.*

TONY'S CREW IS PLANNING SOMETHING *HUGE* OUT THERE, AND THIS IS WHERE WE START TO *FIGHT BACK.*

GUYS, I THINK YOU BETTER *SEE* THIS...

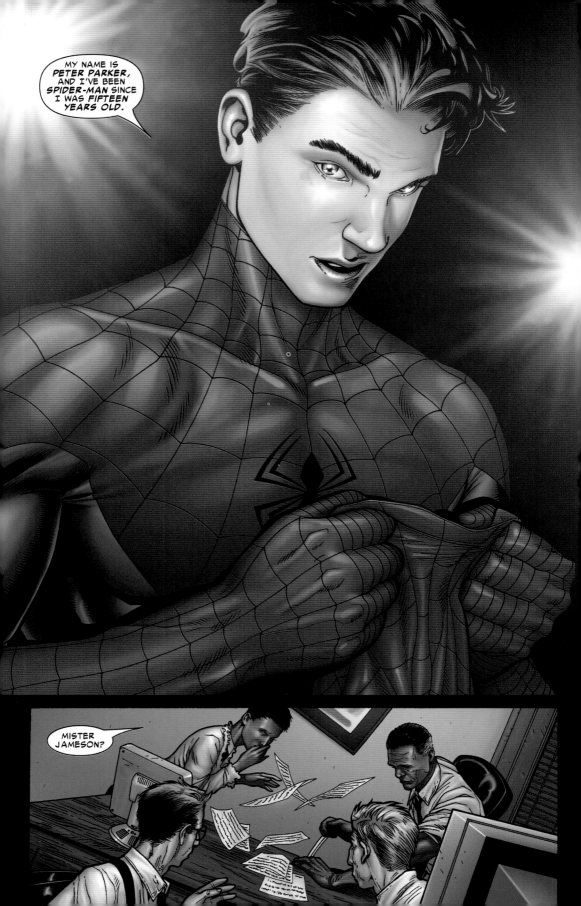

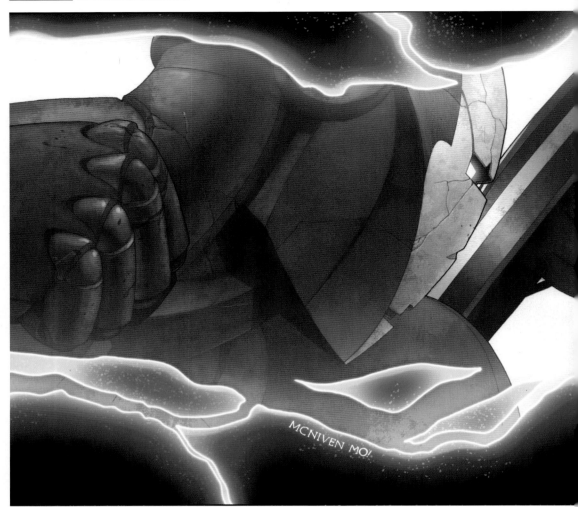

YOU UNMASKED SPIDER-MAN ON *LIVE* TELEVISION?

NO, PARKER UNMASKED *VOLUNTARILY,* T'CHALLA, BECAUSE IRON MAN EXPLAINED THE *GRAVITY* OF OUR SITUATION.

CONFIDENCE IN SUPER-HUMANS IS AT AN *ALL-TIME LOW.* STARK'S PLAN FOR A NEW BEGINNING IS THE ONLY CHANCE WE HAVE LEFT.

A SUPER POLICE FORCE COVERING *ALL FIFTY STATES?* AND ME HELPING HIM HUNT DOWN THE SUPER HEROES WHO *DISAGREE* WITH IT?

I DON'T THINK SO, REED. WE DON'T LIKE IT WHEN AMERICA INTERFERES IN WAKANDAN AFFAIRS, AND I CAN ONLY ASSUME THE FEELING IS *RECIPROCATED.*

ACTUALLY, THE PRESIDENT REQUESTED THIS OF YOU *PERSONALLY...*

WELL, I'M AFRAID HE'S GOING TO BE *DISAPPOINTED.* NOW TELL ME: WHAT ABOUT JOHNNY STORM? IS THE HUMAN TORCH RECOVERING *WELL?*

I HAVEN'T CHECKED IN FOR A DAY OR TWO, BUT SUSAN'S BARELY LEFT HIS BEDSIDE. IF ANYTHING WAS WRONG, I'M SURE I'D HAVE *HEARD.*

I *LOVE* IT OUT HERE, DON'T YOU? THIS HIGH-TECH JUNGLE.

IT'S SO *EERIE* STANDING AMONG TREES WITHOUT *BIRDS* OR *INSECTS.*

I'VE ALWAYS MEANT TO ASK: DOES THE ECO-SYSTEM ADAPT ITSELF OR HAVE YOU MANIPULATED IT *ARTIFICIALLY?*

WORD OF ADVICE, REED.

CALL SUSAN.

CAP'S "SECRET AVENGERS" SMASH NEW SINISTER SIX PLOT

Boston Star

DOCTOR STRANGE, GREENWICH VILLAGE:

I'M SORRY, YELLOWJACKET, BUT THE MASTER SAID HE WOULDN'T EVEN *CONSIDER* SUPPORTING TONY STARK'S PLANS.

IN FACT, HE'S GONE INTO SECLUSION IN HIS ARCTIC LODGE IN THE HOPE THAT HE MIGHT *RESOLVE* YOUR DIFFERENCES BY *FASTING* FOR FORTY NIGHTS.

WELL, HE KNOWS WHERE TO FIND US IF HE CHANGES HIS MIND, WONG.

DAMN WATCH *ALWAYS* SEEMS TO STOP WHEN I'M IN THIS STUPID HOUSE.

The Chronicle

TONY STARK PROMISES TO TACKLE SUPER-REBELS

JUST HOW MANY HEROES ARE IN HIS NEW TEAM?

THIS MUST BE THE FIRST TIME YOU AND I HAVE BEEN ALONE SINCE *MARRAKESH*, MISS FROST.

TELL ME: DOES CYCLOPS KNOW ABOUT THAT LITTLE ARRANGEMENT WE USED TO HAVE WHEN NEITHER OF US WERE DATING?

OH, CYCLOPS KNOWS *EVERYTHING*, TONY. HE CAN'T KEEP SECRETS FROM MY TELEPATHIC MIND, SO IT'S ONLY FAIR THAT I DON'T KEEP ANYTHING FROM *HIM*.

MY. YOU REALLY *HAVE* CHANGED.

OBVIOUSLY, YOU KNOW WHAT I'M ABOUT TO ASK. IS THERE ANY *POINT* IN *VERBALIZING*?

NOT ESPECIALLY. WE HAD A MEETING JUST LAST NIGHT AND DECIDED THAT HELPING YOU HUNT DOWN THESE ANTI-REGISTRATION REBELS WOULD BE A VIOLATION OF EVERYTHING THE X-MEN *BELIEVE* IN.

IT'S A S.H.I.E.L.D. ELECTRON-SCRAMBLER. DEVELOPED BY NICK FURY'S TECH TEAM IN CASE YOU EVER WENT OVER TO THE OTHER SIDE.

AAAGH!

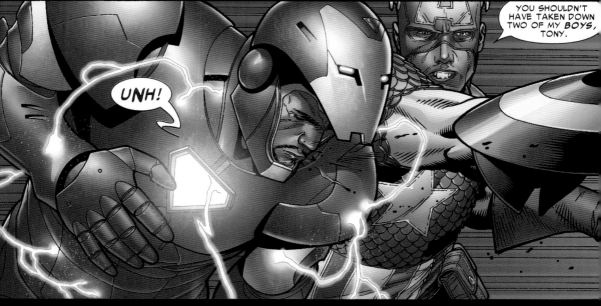

UNH!

YOU SHOULDN'T HAVE TAKEN DOWN TWO OF MY BOYS, TONY.

HEAD FOR THE WATER!

GO!!

HANK, PLEASE! WE CAN DO THIS WITHOUT YOU HAVING TO GROW--!

NOT TO MENTION THAT *"BUTT-KICKING"* BUTTON.

...RMOR, REROUTE ...RIMARY POWER SYSTEMS AND REBOOT.

REROUTING.

REBOOT.

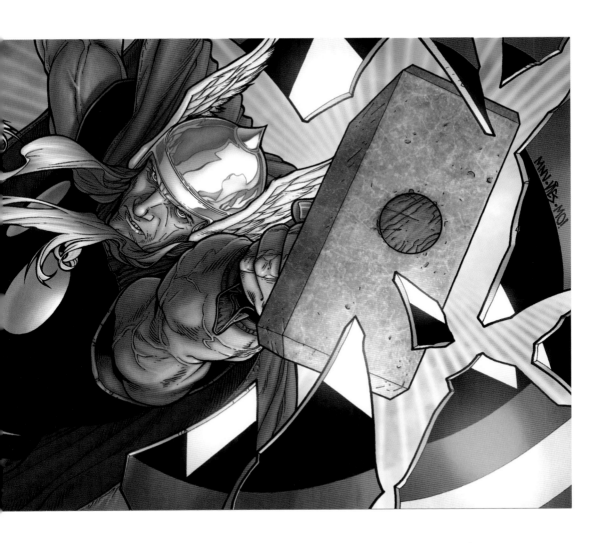

THOR, WHAT ARE YOU DOING? IT'S ME, MAN. THE FALCON...

WHERE HAVE YOU *BEEN?* EVERYBODY THOUGHT YOU WERE DEAD.

NO, DAGGER. THAT WOULD BE *YOU.*

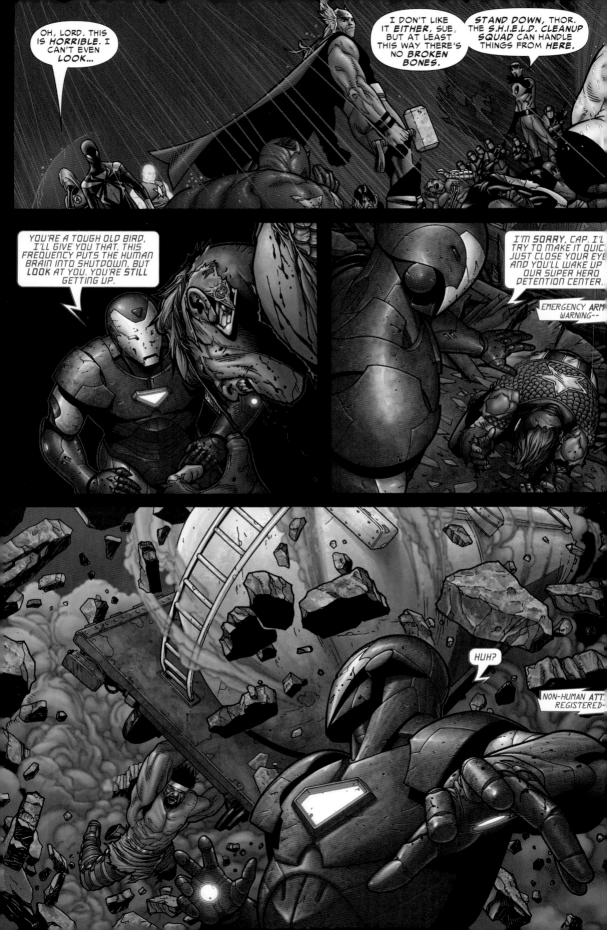

SOMEBODY SWITCHED IT OFF!

SO WHAT ARE YOU WAITING FOR?

UNGH!

AVENGERS TOWER:

GOLIATH'S FUNERAL, NEW JERSEY:

HELL OF A SEND-OFF, GIVEN THE CIRCUMSTANCES.

GUY WAS A SUPER HERO, HAPPY, AND HE SAVED A LOT OF LIVES OVER THE YEARS. THAT'S SOMETHING WE CAN'T FORGET NO MATTER HOW BAD THIS GETS.

JUST A SHAME THEY COULDN'T SHRINK HIM DOWN. I WONDER HOW MUCH HIS FAMILY HAD TO SHELL OUT FOR THESE THIRTY-EIGHT BURIAL PLOTS.

NOTHING. I TOOK CARE OF ALL THE EXPENSES. IT WAS THE LEAST I COULD DO...

IS IT JUST *ME*
OR IS PETER PARKER
ACTING VERY, VERY
SUSPICIOUSLY?

My darling Reed...

*I know Johnny's out of the
hospital and the family's
back together again. I know
I should be happy, but
I'm not.*

*I'm so ASHAMED of you
right now, and ashamed of
myself for supporting your
fascistic plans. I hate what
I've become, and that's why
I'm joining Cap's SECRET
AVENGERS team.*

*Please understand:
This is not another
cry for attention.
This is not me trying
to distract you from
your all-important
work.*

*This is because our hands are soaked in Bill
Foster's BLOOD and you're so blinded by your
graphs and social projections that you can't
even SEE it.*

SO HOW MANY OF OUR GUYS ARE WE *LOSING?*

MORE THAN WE CAN AFFORD. A COUPLE OF CAP'S PEOPLE ARE TALKING ABOUT COMING OVER, BUT THE BALANCE HAS DEFINITELY TIPPED IN THEIR *FAVOR* AFTER THIS.

MAYBE WE COULD JUST BRING FORWARD THIS *FIFTY STATE INITIATIVE* THING. WOULDN'T THESE *NEW* HEROES BE ABLE TO GET THINGS UNDER CONTROL AGAIN?

YEAH, BUT THEY'RE STILL AT LEAST A MONTH AWAY FROM BEING FINISHED. WE NEED TO MOVE FAST AND WE NEED PEOPLE WITH EXPERIENCE IN *SUPERHUMAN* COMBAT...

YOU MEAN THIS LATEST ITERATION OF *THE THUNDERBOLTS* YOU'VE ASSEMBLED?

AFTER WHAT JUST WENT DOWN, IT'S THE ONLY COURSE OF ACTION WE'VE GOT *LEFT*, JAN.

I SHOULD STRESS THAT THEIR INVOLVEMENT IS *STRICTLY TEMPORARY.* THIS IS JUST TO CAPTURE *CAP'S TEAM*, AND THEY'LL ALL GO BACK TO JAIL *IMMEDIATELY* AFTERWARDS.

EACH AND EVERY ONE OF THEM WILL BE *CHIPPED AND TAGGED*, THEIR EVERY MOVEMENT MONITORED BY *MICROSCOPIC NANOBOTS.*

WELL, THEY DON'T EXACTLY LOOK *THRILLED* ABOUT THE PROSPECT OF TEAMING UP WITH *THE AVENGERS...*

WHAT YOU NEED TO **APPRECIATE** IS THAT THERE ARE FORCES WITHIN **S.H.I.E.L.D.** AND THE GOVERNMENT WHO WOULD LIKE NOTHING MORE THAN TO ABSOLUTELY **OUTLAW** ALL SUPERHUMANS!

THE COMPROMISE WE OFFERED THEM WAS **REGULATING** OUR BEHAVIOR! BECAUSE GOING BACK TO THE **GOOD OLD DAYS** WAS NEVER ON THE TABLE, PETER!

GET OUT OF MY WAY...

DON'T BE A FOOL! YOU REALLY THINK YOU CAN JUST GO BACK TO YOUR OLD LIFE NOW THAT EVERYONE KNOWS WHO YOU ARE?

THIS ISN'T JUST ABOUT YOU ANYMORE! WHAT ABOUT MAY? WHAT ABOUT MARY JANE?

32nd STREET:

YOU THINK THEY SAW US?

EVEN IF THEY DID, WHAT'S THERE TO SEE? WE'RE NOT THE HUMAN TORCH AND THE INVISIBLE WOMAN ANYMORE. WE'RE MR. AND MRS. *RYAN LANDAU* AND WE'RE OUT FOR A MIDNIGHT STROLL.

I'M STILL ANNOYED NICK FURY COULDN'T FIND US ANY *BROTHER AND SISTER* IDENTITIES. PRETENDING WE'RE A MARRIED COUPLE IS THE CREEPIEST THING I'VE EVER DONE.

HOW DO YOU THINK I FEEL, SIS? YOU LOOK LIKE MY LAST DATE'S *GRANDMOTHER...*

STILL, IT LETS US GET OUT THERE TO HELP PEOPLE, AND THAT'S WHAT'S *IMPORTANT*, RIGHT?

CAPTAIN AMERICA'S NEW H.Q.:

TAKE IT EASY, GUYS. IT'S ONLY JOHNNY AND SUE BACK FROM A *MISSION.*

THIS IS HORRIBLE.

THE *PUBLIC'S* BEHIND US, THE *GOVERNMENT'S* BEHIND US, CRIME IS AT AN *ALL-TIME LOW*. WHY ARE OUR *OWN PEOPLE* THE ONLY ONES CAUSING *PROBLEMS*, JENNIFER?

SOMETIMES I WISH WE'D NEVER GOTTEN *INVOLVED*. DO YOU EVER STOP TO THINK HOW MUCH *EASIER* THINGS WOULD BE IF WE HADN'T SPLICED THOR'S DNA WITH HANK PYM'S *CYBER-TECH?*

IF WE DIDN'T HAVE THIS BIG FINAL BATTLE PLANNED WITH ALL THOSE *THUNDERBOLT LUNATICS?*

2 TO GO LIVE AT THE EXCELSIOR

HANK WOULDN'T BE DOPED-UP ON *ANTI-DEPRESSANTS* AND MY DARLING SUE WOULD NEVER HAVE *LEFT...*

MAYBE NOT. BUT PUBLIC OPINION WOULD HAVE FORCED S.H.I.E.L.D. TO BRING DOWN EVERY *SUPER HERO* IN AMERICA.

PEOPLE WERE SICK OF SIXTEEN-YEAR-OLD KIDS *BLOWING UP BUILDINGS,* REED.

YOU GUYS GAVE US ALL A *FUTURE.*

YOU HAVE TO UNDERSTAND WHY WE'RE *DOING* THIS, DAREDEVIL. WE DON'T TAKE ANY PLEASURE IN HUNTING DOWN OUR *FRIENDS*.

WE'RE BACKING THESE REFORMS BECAUSE THE ONLY OTHER OPTION IS A *COMPLETE BAN* ON ALL *SUPER HEROES*. AND NOBODY WANTS *THAT* TO HAPPEN, RIGHT?

GATEWAY IS ACTIVE! PROCEEDING THROUGH!

OUR BIG IDEA IS FIFTY SUPER-TEAMS SPREAD OVER ALL FIFTY STATES, EACH ONE LICENSED AND ACCOUNTABLE TO THE TAXPAYER.

IT'S THE NEXT STAGE IN SUPERHUMAN EVOLUTION: A *FEDERAL FORCE* FROM *COAST-TO-COAST*.

THE NEGATIVE ZONE:

WE'VE BEEN WORKING ON THIS FOR MONTHS, CREATING NEW SUPER HEROES AND REVAMPING ANYONE WHO WANTS TO *JOIN* US.

NATURALLY, YOU'D BE AT THE TOP OF OUR LIST IF YOU WERE INTERESTED. YOU COULD EVEN HAVE YOUR OWN TEAM.

CAN WE STILL CALL HIM HERCULES WHEN THERE'S *ALREADY* A HERCULES OUT THERE?

FORTUNATELY, GREEK GODS AREN'T ESPECIALLY *LITIGIOUS*, COMMANDER HILL. BESIDES, ALL THOSE GOLIATHS OVER THE YEARS NEVER BOTHERED *ME*.

THE BAXTER BUILDING:

CAPTAIN AMERICA'S SAFEHOUSE:

OKAY, I'M IN THEIR *DATA-HOUSE.*

GOOD. NOW I NEED EVERYTHING YOU CAN FIND ON THIS NUMBER 42 COMPLEX: THIS BIG SUPER-PRISON WHERE THEY'RE HOLDING OUR GUYS IN THE NEGATIVE ZONE.

I NEED THE *SIZE,* HOW MUCH SPACE WE'LL HAVE TO *MOVE* AROUND AND HOW MANY *ACCESS POINTS* THEY'VE BUILT. THINK YOU CAN HANDLE THAT WITHOUT SHOOTING SOMEBODY IN THE *HEAD?*

HILARIOUS.

UH-OH.

WHAT'S UP?

THIS COMPOUND'S GOT MORE PROTECTION THAN ANYTHING I EVER SAW. WE'RE GONNA NEED A LOT MORE THAN YOUR TEAM OF *GRUNTS* TO SPRING THESE GUYS.

I'M *ON IT,* CASTLE.

JUST KEEP *TYPING.*

STAMFORD, CONNECTICUT:

I HOPE YOU LIKE THE GARDENS WE BUILT IN THE *CHILDREN'S HONOR*, MIRIAM.

THEY'RE *BEAUTIFUL*, TONY. SO NICE TO HAVE A PLACE WHERE WE CAN COME AND SIT--Y'KNOW-- WHENEVER WE'RE FEELING *LONELY* AND STUFF.

I REALLY WANT TO THANK YOU FOR ALL THIS. NOT JUST THE MONEY. I MEAN, ALL THE WORK YOU'VE DONE TO PUSH MY *BIG IDEA*.

I *HATE* HOW MUCH IT'S COST YOU PERSONALLY. I NEVER WOULD HAVE *ASKED* IF I'D KNOWN YOUR LIVES WOULD GET TORN APART LIKE THIS.

WE KNEW WHAT WE WERE *TAKING ON*, MIRIAM. THERE'S NO SHAME IN MAKING ENEMIES IF IT MEANS MAKING PEOPLE *SAFER*.

DR. STRANGE'S SANCTUARY, THE NORTH POLE:

HOW LONG SINCE YOU HAVE EATEN NOW, STEPHEN STRANGE?

JUST A LITTLE WATER SINCE THE CIVIL WAR BEGAN, UATU.

ARE YOU NOT TEMPTED TO SIMPLY *END* IT? WITH YOUR GREAT POWER, YOU COULD STOP THIS QUARREL WITH A *GESTURE* OR A *WHISPER*.

PRECISELY WHY I MUST REMAIN ABOVE THE FRAY.

THERE IS NO RIGHT OR WRONG IN THIS DEBATE. IT IS SIMPLY A MATTER OF *PERSPECTIVE*, AND IT IS NOT MY PLACE TO INFLUENCE THE EVOLUTION OF *THE SUPERHUMAN ROLE*.

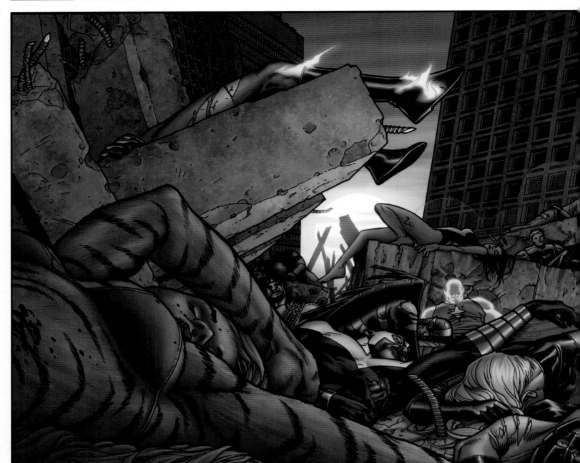

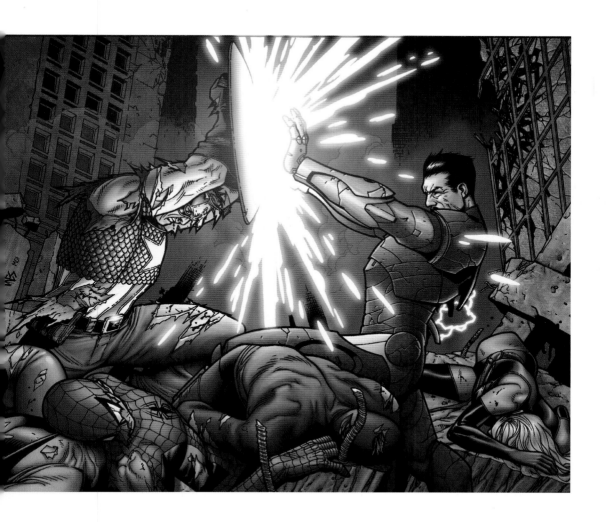

OUTSIDE THE BAXTER BUILDING,
NEW YORK:

ALL THE FLYERS, GRAB A FRIEND!

NOW!

OH MY GOD.

WHAT'S WRONG?

THEY'RE RIGHT. WE'RE NOT FIGHTING FOR THE PEOPLE ANYMORE, FA-CON...

LOOK AT US.

WE'RE JUST FIGHTING.

MY DEAR, SWEET SUSAN:

FORGIVE MY ERRATIC HANDWRITING. YOU KNOW HOW DIFFICULT I FIND SLOWING MY THOUGHTS TO A SPEED WHERE THE HUMAN HAND CAN TRANSLATE MY SENTIMENTS INTO LINEAR SENTENCES.

IT HAS BEEN TWO WEEKS NOW SINCE THAT TERRIBLE BATTLE AND I WAS PLEASED TO SEE THAT YOU ACCEPTED THE GENERAL HERO AMNESTY GIVEN IN THE WAKE OF CAPTAIN AMERICA'S *SURRENDER.*

EN OUR CONTROVERSIAL PRISON IN THE NEGATIVE
ONE WAS MET WITH RAPTUROUS APPLAUSE WHEN WE
NALLY WENT PUBLIC.

OW **FRIGHTENING** THE WORLD MUST HAVE
EEMED BEFORE THIS: VIGILANTES, AMATEURS,
UPER-VILLAINS BROODING IN CELLS THAT
EVER SEEMED TO **HOLD** THEM.

HE ONLY SURPRISE IS
OW WE WERE **TOLERATED**
OR AS LONG AS WE **WERE**.

F COURSE, IT WOULD BE
LIE TO SUGGEST THAT
VERYONE IS HAPPY WITH
UR NEW ARRANGEMENT.

SOME HAVE MOVED TO
CANADA IN THE HOPE OF
A MORE **OLD-SCHOOL**
CAREER...

WHILE A SMALL BAND
F CAP'S FOLLOWERS
EMAIN RADICALIZED IN
HE **UNDERGROUND**
OVEMENT.

DIG
THE OUTFIT,
MAN.

THANKS.

NOT TO MENTION
CAPTAIN AMERICA
HIMSELF...

THE S.H.I.E.L.D. HELICARRIER, FIVE MILES OVER NEW YORK CITY:

DIRECTOR OF S.H.I.E.L.D.?

WHY NOT, MRS. SHARPE? AS A MAN WITH CLOSE LINKS TO BOTH THE GOVERNMENT AND THE SUPERHUMAN COMMUNITY, I THINK IT MAKES PERFECT SENSE, IF NICK FURY'S STILL AMONG THE MISSING.

UH, COULD WE HAVE A COUPLE OF *COFFEES* OVER HERE, PLEASE, *DEPUTY COMMANDER HILL?* CREAM AND PLENTY OF SUGAR?

CIVIL
WAR

BY MICHAEL
TURNER
& ASPEN

CIVIL WAR #1

CIVIL WAR #2

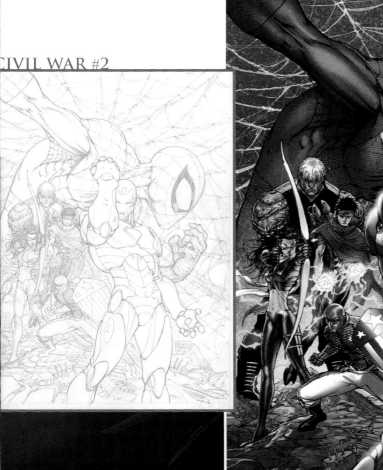

CIVIL WAR #3

THE GREATEST COMIC EVENTS
FROM THE HOUSE OF IDEAS!

**Marvel Super Heroes:
Secret Wars**
ISBN: 978-1-904159-83-4
Price: £14.99

House of M
ISBN: 978-1-905239-22-1
Price: £14.99

Secret War
ISBN: 978-1-905239-16-0
Price: £14.99

Planet Hulk Omnibus
ISBN: 978-1-905239-66-5
Price: £14.99

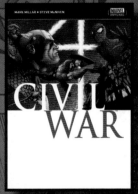

Civil War
ISBN: 978-1-905239-60-3
Price: £10.99

World War Hulk
ISBN: 978-1-905239-77-4
Price: £14.99

Secret Invasion
ISBN: 978-1-84653-405-8
Price: £14.99

Captain America Reborn
ISBN: 978-1-84653-440-9
Price: £14.99

Siege
ISBN: 978-1-84653-452-2
Price: £12.99

Avengers Prime
ISBN: 978-1-84653-480-5
Price: £11.99

Fear Itself
ISBN: 978-1-84653-494-2
Price: £15.99

**Avengers:
The Children's Crusade**
ISBN: 978-1-84653-485-0
Price: £16.99